MICROSOFT TEAMS FOI

A Complete Beginner's Guide to Mastering Office
365 Microsoft Teams for Online Learning and
Classroom Management

Annie Stevens

TABLE OF CONTENTS

Introduction..1

    Why Should Your Business Use Microsoft Teams?..........................4

Chapter 1: Understanding Of Distance And Remote Learning..........6

How Is Distance Learning Different From Regular Learning?........11

Chapter 2: Microsoft Teams And Teaching 14

    Microsoft Teams For The Classroom 16

How Does Microsoft Teams Work?..17

For Teachers: Microsoft Teams Step-By-Step Tutorial 20

1. Installation 20

2. Creating A Team...20

3. [Prior To Lesson] Other Useful Tools To Setup...........................20

4. [Prior To Lesson] Priming Your Students....................................21

5. Starting A "Meeting" (Video Call) 21

6. Checklist During The Call..21

7. Taking Attendance..22

8. [Post Lesson] Feedback, Checks For Understanding 22

Key Features..23

    Communication And Collaboration 23

Assignments 23

    App Integrations...24

How Teams Can Change Learning 24

Your Microsoft Teams Classroom: 25

Understanding Microsoft Teams Channels 25

    Microsoft Teams Channel Permissions:..26

    Ways Teachers Can Use Channels In Teams – As An Asset For A
    Larger Class 26

Don't Forget:..27

Chapter 3: Uses And Importance Of Microsoft Team For Education And Business 28

Things You Should Know About Microsoft Teams...........29

Why Educational Institutions Need To Use Microsoft Teams..........32

Online Learning Can't Replace Classrooms. Microsoft Teams Wants To Change That 34

New Features Support The Digital Transformation............35

The Challenges And Science Of Online-Learning 36

Teams Are Getting Features That Go Beyond Education...................37

Chapter 4: Creative Ways Of Using Microsoft Teams......38

Microsoft Teams Leader Attribution 42

Chapter 5: Best Apps And Strategies............................43

Flipgrid 43

Flipgrid's New Features...44

Wakelet 46

Submit A Student Information Center 47

Enable Collaboration Of Students In Group Projects 47

Share The Team's Strengths And Ideas 47

Simplify Your Six-Month Strategy..................................48

Nearpod..48

How To Shake Nearpod In That Presentation 48

How To Interrupt The Microsoft Live Class Session 49

How To Start Your Nearpod Presentation 49

Pear Deck..50

Classroom Suggestions For The Use Of Pear Decks........50

Have A Platform For Students And Let Them Explore......50

Planner..51

What Is Microsoft Planner?..51

Why Join Teams And Managers In Microsoft? 52

Integrating Microsoft Planner With Teams.........................53

Chapter 6: Pros And Cons **55**

Key Elements 55

Equipment 55

Networks 55

Windows Tabs...56

Pros...**56**

Cons...**58**

The Benefits Of Microsoft Teams.......................................**60**

Advantages...**61**

Disadvantages **63**

The Pros And Cons Of Microsoft Teams Vs. Zoom...........**66**

Conclusion..**68**

INTRODUCTION

Microsoft teams' whole ordeal is removing emails from the workplace and serving as the main contact channel. You can chat, share files, host or accept conference calls without leaving the app. You can use MS Teams to do so. Teams offer unrivaled integration with Office 365 as a Microsoft product, so you don't even need to switch apps when working with Office documents. You will instantly generate and share your feedback on the dashboard. Microsoft has put a range of security and protection upgrades to protect the user's privacy and prevent unauthorized users from reading messages or attending meetings.

Fig. Microsoft Team APP

Of course, there are plenty of options to choose from. But Microsoft Teams stands out as one particularly useful solution. And with Office 365, it's entirely free.

Microsoft Teams is a chat-based network complete with document sharing, online meetings, and many other highly useful business communications features. Getting an ample workspace is a secret to being able to make strategic choices and connect with the colleagues. Shared workspace software makes this much easier to do, mainly if a specific team is located in a large organization, has a large number of remote workers, or is made up of a large number of team members.

Microsoft Teams has several main components that make it stand out from other softwares:

- Teams as a form of communication: Teams is made up of networks that are discussion boards between teammates.

- Link and team discussions: Every team member can access and connect to different conversations on the General Channel and can use the @ feature to invite other members to various exchanges.

- It's a chat app: The introductory chat feature is commonly found in most communication apps and can be performed between teams, groups, and individuals.

- You can store Documents in SharePoint: Any team that uses Microsoft Teams will have a SharePoint Online site that contains a default software library folder. All files exchanged through all messages will be transferred to this folder automatically. Permissions and security options can also be customized for sensitive information.

- Internet video call and screen sharing: Enjoy smooth and fast video calls with employees in your company or clients outside of your company. It's awesome to have a successful video call feature on a collaboration platform. You can also enjoy easy and quick desktop sharing for technical assistance and multi-user collaboration.

- Meetings on the web: This feature will help boost interactions, company-wide meetings, and even training with the aid of online meetings that can host up to 10,000 people. Meetings may involve anyone outside or inside a company. Also, this feature includes scheduling, a note-taking function, file sharing, and chat messaging in-meeting.

- Conference Recording: This is a functionality that you will not find in a lot of similar platforms. Anyone can attend an online meeting over the phone with audio conferencing. With a dial-in number covering hundreds of cities, even users will participate on the go without having internet. Notice this requires further licensing.

- Complete phone number: The days of searching for VoIP vendors and ending up overspending on a phone system are over. Microsoft Teams will fully replace the current telephone system in your company. Notice this requires further licensing too.

To put it plainly, Microsoft Teams is conceptually similar to Slack's popular collaboration platform with far more bells and whistles. Plus, Office 365 offers Microsoft Teams for free.

Why Should Your Business Use Microsoft Teams?

Companies can use Microsoft Teams because it is incredibly user-friendly and can make the work experience simpler for remote users or large businesses. Microsoft Teams may be used for projects, outputs, and other business components.

In the case of organizations currently using Skype for Business, the Teams app will replace the Skype app, but all the existing features will stay the same.

Using Microsoft Teams

Teams is extremely quick and user-friendly. There is little to no setup needed. Still, some consideration should be given to how a business needs to use the platform before it is rolled out across the organization.

There are two key choices for consideration:

- "Free for all" approach. Businesses can choose to automatically introduce Microsoft Teams in a "Free for All" manner, where anyone in the business can do anything they want with the software, and the usage and use of the Teams model will evolve organically.

- The Controlled Approaches. This more controlled approach includes the use of Microsoft Teams for particular aspects of the business. It also includes closely restricting who is allowed to use it and who can do certain actions inside it, resulting in a staggered roll-out strategy around the company.

Team members may be provided with training, but excellent online user training materials from Microsoft are also available. These materials are presented as a series of very short videos on how various things can be done and how team functions can be carried out. Due to the easy and simple exchange of documents in teams involving multiple or all members, the platform provides custom training materials and guidance for new users and employees.

The team is a powerful and extremely useful collaboration environment that will only become more popular. Microsoft Teams is included in Office 365 free of charge so that any Office user can benefit from this collaboration solution. In summary, it makes teamwork simple by collaborating, sharing, communicating, and doing everything on a single platform.

CHAPTER 1
UNDERSTANDING OF DISTANCE AND REMOTE LEARNING

In our country, the shockwaves and impacts of COVID-19 are significant, and the shift to distance learning is a major change. School-aged children stay at home, and some families are responsible for facilitating distance learning. But what is distance learning, and how are we going to do it well?

Fig. Distance and remote learning

It's new for students who go to traditional "brick-and-mortar" schools, but we have been using it in education for decades. It is synonymous with online learning, e-learning, or distance education when students are separated from their teachers through online communication. But the difference between online learning and distance learning is that students can still use online learning programs under the supervision of the teacher, where distance learning is physically estranged from the teacher.

Types of Distance Learning

School districts across the country are trying to adapt to this new circumstance, but what type of distance learning is best for them? Here are some various types that they can consider:

Fixed Schedule Online Learning

This is the most frequent type of distance learning in which students log in at a specific time on a platform. Online ESL teachers such as VIPKID will use fixed-time online learning, as students and teachers decide on the time they want to have lessons. The students benefit from this form of learning because they have some deciding power, but it lacks flexibility.

Video Conferencing

An instructor, a student, or a complete school can do a videoconference. Teachers can mute people so that the instructor can chat or pick students in conversation to exchange ideas. Video conferences have chat boxes where teachers can pause and ask students to type their answers to ensure all students are doing the work. During COVID-19, many teachers give virtual classes for their students on platforms such as Zoom at specified times. This is an example of a classroom with a fixed-time video lecture.

Open Schedule Online Learning

This form of online learning is the timeliest and is what many schools plan to introduce during this COVID-19 distance learning period for high school and college students. Students are given deadlines for applications, but at their own speed, they may use various online resources. Students who enjoy freedom or have problems with their concentration excel on these distance learning schedules.

Hybrid Online Learning

Online hybrid or mixed learning combines conventional learning environments and online learning. Students may do most of their training online but have to meet weekly or monthly with their class in person. This form of learning structure allows students to prepare in person for classroom discussions and tests in a timely manner to complete the course work.

Advantages of Distance Learning

Accessibility and Flexibility

The value of distance learning is huge. Students can use any electronic device to access their school rooms, content, virtual classrooms and more. Students have access to the content and will, at any time in the future, return to these materials. For instance, if a student gets ill and loses a couple of weeks of school, these lessons are lost. However, if the student uses distance learning, the lessons can be saved on the various platforms and studied at the convenience of the students. The education of students with learning disabilities will also improve. Students that are over-stimulated by a broad group of students can choose a better environment to succeed. Students who tend to have a hard time concentrating will take breaks and cut the lessons into manageable pieces.

Enhancing Traditional Educational Methods

One of the greatest benefits of distance learning is to have highly skilled professionals who have the ability to communicate remotely with others worldwide. You have only access to the teachers at school and maybe one to five teachers you communicate with every day during the lessons. Distance learning gives education providers the opportunity, through online tours, resources, and conversations, to connect their students with highly qualified professionals, other learning communities, and locations. Currently, we are experiencing a flood of free, virtual field trips to zoos and aquariums throughout the world. Students will visit places where they will never have the opportunity to travel to and learn more about subjects they really are interested in learning. The teachers use virtual field excursions in traditional classrooms as a way to improve students' curricula. Many families profit from these amazing opportunities to help manage their time or distance learning at home.

Secondary or Postsecondary Education Benefits

Distance learning has been used by schools and higher education due to its many advantages. Students will "earn as they learn" by joining full-time jobs and graduating on-line. It also saves time and money so that students don't need to go to college.

Challenges of Distance Learning

Distractions Take Away from Learning

Self-discipline is an important skill to have if you want to learn successfully. Other social media sites, people, or their environments may distract students easily. Try to create a learning environment that is free of physical obstacles. Setting a timer and allowing breaks can enable students to remain completely active throughout distance learning.

Technology Issues

Accessibility is a significant benefit of online learning but can be highly disadvantageous if families do not have access to technology. There could be major problems if there are difficulties with equipment or communications or if the student or family is not technologically skilled. During this COVID-19 time, educators aim to provide family members with computers, send simple messages so that families can understand clearly, and give families time to gather materials from their buildings for physical learning.

Quality of Learning

The best teaching is high-quality training. Such classes are not suitable for strict online teaching. Some teachers who provide distance learning courses may not be the best or highly qualified. The instructor may be the best teacher, but online platforms are not the easiest and most convenient way to teach. We now see thousands of teachers who were not educated or taught online do so.

Districts need to explain which distance learning system their teachers want to use and which tools are required to enable teachers to concentrate their time and energy on these instruments. In order to ensure our students' learning and to flourish in this period, our contact between teachers' administrators and their families must be transparent, simple, consistent, and solution-oriented. We need to navigate across these new waters of learning distance during this pandemic as a global educational culture.

How Is Distance Learning Different from Regular Learning?

The difference between distance education and normal education is focused on the existence of a student or teacher. But precisely, what does it mean?

Most of this translates into increased flexibility for students and instructors, but the successful completion of the course often involves higher degrees of discipline and preparation.

The increased flexibility of remote learning is most apparent since students can select courses according to their schedules and resources. And in the case of interactive education, students can also choose which teaching methods best suited to their needs. (Teachers should do the same.)

However, the flip side of independence is the discipline needed to learn successfully. In order to get the work done, students need to motivate themselves, especially for systems that do not require them to be present at a particular time or location.

However, in some situations, distance learning is not only appropriate, but it is the best choice. Even remote education has its benefits.

Features to Look for in a Distance Learning System

Regardless of whether you are an instructor or a student, certain features are required to make the most of a remote learning environment.

Ease of Use

The secret is a simplification. Any method you follow to teach or learn should be easy to use for those concerned. This involves a direct link and a variety of key features, including:

- Digital annotation and whiteboarding
- Screen recording and audio
- Sharing and Media creation
- Multi-device compatibility
- Direct student-to-teacher communication

Accreditation

The reputation of a distance learning program is a mixture of the teacher and the network. It is necessary for students to remember what they are getting out of this. Is it an acknowledged degree? A credential professional? A completion certificate? All these things should be recalled before you file.

And it is necessary for educators to learn what kind of accreditation the system can offer on your behalf or on behalf of their school to implement a remote learning system. Recognition by outside bodies is mandatory for advanced degrees or professional qualifications.

Timetable

The course schedule is very relevant to their material and not to the framework, as most distance learning programs are designed to be fairly versatile in this regard. However, when choosing a course, it is an important aspect to remember.

Is the path synchronous or asynchronous? Are there any deadlines? How long would the whole course take to be completed? And does the program fit your software?

Online teaching obviously isn't a magic wand, and classroom learning will still be necessary. At the same time, the opportunity for distance learning to link educators and learners in a different way still has untapped potential. Its future appears to be complex, ranging from increased versatility to new learning styles.

CHAPTER 2

MICROSOFT TEAMS AND TEACHING

I t is an online collaboration network for teachers and students, allowing video-chat, document-sharing, collaborative editing, and much more.

Fig. Microsoft teams

Clearly, Microsoft Teams does not pretend to be a Learning Management System or plan to replace the current LMS in a school. It is designed to contribute to the growth of this framework, to improve the teaching of educators, and to allow students to participate more both in and outside of the classroom.

The intention of this chapter is to explain what Teams is, how it functions, and how teachers and students can use it as an online learning platform.

Microsoft Teams was originally introduced as a business portal and has undergone several changes and upgrades. As you would probably understand, Microsoft Education teams use the same general framework for free access, which anyone can use and which can only be personalized to schools.

The platform provides an online space for teachers and students, including occasional third parties, to exchange information, lectures, meetings, assignments, and applications.

Teachers may build classes within a class, which may be an entire class or subgroup. They can also create larger groups, for instance, in the math, committee, or club department.

Among those groups, resources can be exchanged, project members can collaborate, and tasks can be set up and communicated live through the Class Notebook. SharePoint is a useful folder structure that stores all shared files automatically, which can be used in other locations, such as chat.

Chat is another major function that makes it possible to talk about the lesson in real-time. But there is also video chat with whole classes or individual talks.

The surface was scratched to get a little insight into how Microsoft's education teams can be used.

What devices does Microsoft Teams work with?

There is a host that deals with Microsoft teams when it comes to compatible devices. Microsoft devices would probably be the most apparent and most generally available. So, stuff such as the two-in-one laptop-tablet by Microsoft Surface is great options for running Windows OS on a touch screen.

Also, any Windows machine that is up to date will run Teams well.

Teams can be used on iOS and Android phones and tablets since their website is online, and apps are available. It's going to work even on Linux.

Check out Microsoft hardware requirements for the whole list of compatible devices and how efficient they have to be.

How much does Microsoft Teams cost?

In its most simple form, Microsoft teams is free. This limits your per-capita capacity to 2 GB with a typical storage space of up to 10 GB. However, it is a feasible alternative with limitless video chat.

Apps including Outlook, Phrase, PowerPoint, Excel, and OneNote are included in Office 365 A1's models.

To sign up for the full edition of the teams as part of Office 365 A3, pricing begins with an annual commitment of $2.50 per user per month. The above applications and web apps and additional management and security software are included.

Microsoft Teams for the classroom

Microsoft Education Teams include unique team forms for use in a school. This type of team Class provides classroom resources like assignments, one notebook, one reading material folder, and the ability to mute students.

The SDS is another feature of teams that enables the network to be developed by IT departments on a school level. In order for things like class rosters to be preserved and conveniently used within the team structure, the information is already being included in the educational institution's system.

Professors can manually set up their own lessons and add students at any time, using invite codes.

If developed, the team leader (in most cases, the teacher) may change the settings. This includes the possibility of adding a team image, creating a channel for classroom subjects or groups, and adding applications such as Kahoot, Flipgrid, and Quizlet. Then the team should be listed as the first post so that the discussion can begin.

How does Microsoft Teams work?

After forming a team as a class, setting up a class notebook with OneNote is an excellent activity. This provides a place for students to connect and work together and offers a board style.

Fig. Microsoft team working

Next up, build tasks using the top menu tab. This ensures that students will finish the work and turn it in to the date that they have planned.

This can be adapted for use by teams if you have access to the InVision whiteboard.

In order to start a virtual lesson, you must have a "meeting," so you and your students can see and hear each other as you are in the classroom. The blurry background feature is a useful function that helps you to easily conceal your environment and protect your privacy.

Take a call with a calendar case, inviting everyone. You can then view the attendance list by clicking on the top right in the meeting file. This will show the participants – everything laid down in Excel to be saved and referred to as required. It will indicate who, where, and when they have joined.

Think of Microsoft Teams as a platform for interacting online together with your students, a place for chatting, exchanging files, and even online meetings.

Sign-up procedure:

- Select Sign Up Free from product.office.com/Microsoft teams.

- Type your email address with Microsoft and click Next.

- Pick and choose the Next choice.

- Pick Sign in and enter your password.

- Set up your teams, then add the final info.

Essential functions:

- Download and Start

- Build a Team

- [prior to Lecture] Useful setup tools (Invision Whiteboard, Onenote)

- [Prior to Learning] Priming the students

- Launch video calling

- Checklist (Muting students, sharing screen) during the call

- Take attendance

- [Post lesson] Reviews, Comprehension tests

For teachers: Microsoft Teams Step-by-Step Tutorial

It can be rather daunting to get teams up and running for home-based learning for the first time, so this is a quick guide to setting up the essential functions:

1. Installation

The method is identical for windows users — download, install, and launch the software from your application menu (you can also type "Microsoft Teams" into your search bar and add it to your taskbar for easy access afterward).

2. Creating a team

Click on "Teams" in the left sidebar to create a team for your class and then on "Create a team."

3. [Prior to Lesson] Other useful tools to setup

Develop a class notebook (OneNote) — this generates a digital notebook the student can customize.

Creating assignments — students can submit assignments online, and MS Teams can send you a summary of who submitted and who did not (deadlines can be set to restrict submissions).

InVision whiteboard would be a useful companion if you have a tablet:

While the MS Whiteboard is prone to crashing, Freehand by Invision is comparatively stable (tested on two occasions with 20 users). You may also use the screen sharing feature to open a whiteboard when viewing sideways your slides.

4. [Prior to Lesson] Priming your students

In addition to the technological aspects of setting up, students may also need to adapt to the virtual world.

That covers but is not limited to:

- Confirm your students have been assigned to the respective class groups.

- Reminding the students that their distance learning experience should be free of distractions;

- Muting in during the call.

5. Starting a "meeting" (video call)

Click on the Video Camera icon at the bottom of your screen to launch a video call.

6. Checklist during the call

Link a headset to a microphone — the one that's bundled with your smartphone should be enough to make your voice clearer;

"Audio monitor / you can hear me" — confirm that the audio is broadcast from your end;

Internet link / LAN cable-this will increase internet speed and make it more secure such that an unreliable network is less disruptive;

If your network is sluggish / you think your students find the internet sluggish, consider turning off the video for your students;

Mute the speakers in order to reduce background noise. With ambient soundcheck, the chat feature sometimes becomes exponentially noisier (this is our only way to 'see' them and address them if they are muted);

Make sure you display the right screen — usually helps to minimize open windows; using split-screen functions will help create a classroom-like effect.

7. Taking Attendance

Taking part is often one of those boring tasks each teacher faces. It may seem particularly daunting to do online, as students may arrive late or join halfway, and tracking becomes difficult.

Essentially, to get the tracking feature, you need to create a calendar event.

8. [Post Lesson] Feedback, Checks for Understanding

Consider using the class notebooks and the "assignments" tab as a way to check if students were successful in the lesson.

Administer polls using bots such as Polly or just the General Chat feature to receive input from students on the lesson.

Explore other integrated MS team apps that you can use to make your classes easier to administer!

Key features

Communication and collaboration

The teachers and students will interact one-on-one or in groups using the Microsoft Teams platform:

- Teachers will instantly send messages and announcements to specific students or to entire classes.

- Individual users can build chats with other users in private.

- With the function Channels, teachers may create sub-categories for file storage, special assignments, or centered topics within each team.

- Users may use built-in Skype technology to hold video meetings or engage in video discussions with Flipgrid, which is also incorporated right into the app.

- Teachers can use OneNote Class Notebooks to exchange notes and files and provide individual students with input. Also, notebooks may be exchanged between faculty members to gather information, collaborate and create new papers, and exchange materials for professional development.

Assignments

Microsoft recently introduced tools to handle assignments; many of these features come from the Chalkup application that joined Microsoft earlier this year. Teachers can now handle their tasks with this new addition, without ever leaving the Teams area.

Teachers will use the Software for Assignments to:

Create, appoint, collect, and provide input on assignments.

Connect related files — Microsoft Office applications such as Vocabulary, PowerPoint, Excel, and OneNote are built right into the software, so you can build and delegate students to do the same with these applications.

Construct, save, and use rubrics for student job assessment: The rubric creator is flexible and enables users to add written input and go back and edit later. (Microsoft is also working on adding capabilities for a single-point rubric to the tool!)

App integrations

For educators and students who have a subscription to Office 365 Education (which is also available for free), it's all absolutely free.

You can also use Teams on the go: just place the iOS or Android app on your mobile device, and you can access your classroom from anywhere.

How Teams can change learning

With so much of what you need built into one seamless platform, you no longer have to deal with the trouble of mixing your accounts, multiple sign-ins, and toggling back and forth between apps.

Knowing that students can work together in a cohesive atmosphere ensures that you can delegate more collaborative tasks, and you will be able to track how things are going in each group.

Getting everyone educated on a forum where each person can participate at the same level — even quiet students have the opportunity to have an active voice in discussions.

Having a central place for professional learning and collaboration — where you can exchange knowledge and address important issues and initiatives with your colleagues — could mean less time-consuming meetings.

Your Microsoft Teams Classroom:

For your Classroom, think of Microsoft Teams as your learning center for every class you teach, or even after-school events. It is the centrality of your command for each class. If you teach multiple classes, you'll find yourself with multiple teams. You can customize them by clicking on Teams on the left sidebar. There, you'll see all the teams you're part of.

It's crucial that you name your teams.

You want to make sure you are using identifiers so that if there is ever a problem, there are not seven 'Humanities' sections on the backend. Make sure it has distinctive qualities that make it easier for students to find them-and that class names aren't repetitive and confusing.

Understanding Microsoft Teams Channels

Channels are one of the Teams' greatest features, and so many different forms can be used.

Channels are intended to be a shared space where participants can have discussions and work together on classwork and/or projects.

Build a specific 'Meetings' channel to make them easier to find- particularly for the younger ones.

Microsoft Teams Channel Permissions:

You may also adjust the permissions on the channel to allow only a few students to come in – or allow students to help you manage and add content.

You can also use SharePoint to build Folders Only in View. This is critical because all folders remain collaborative in channels, as the norm.

Ways Teachers Can Use Channels in Teams – As An Asset For A Larger Class

- Non-group job-through private networks for community groups;

- Split Channels in Units or Themes;

- Make the Q and A project or investigation areas and the tools;

- College Shared Room with Tutorials;

- Break Down a Unit By Idea Channels – This can get crowded, so suggest hiding or removing it as soon as it's not required;

- Differentiated Content-offer different content to different audiences by developing specific community channels;

- Capital Zone.

Don't Forget:

When you've moved on to new content or concept, you can cover the channel.

Change the notifications for the channel to your preference or alert level.

You may add additional tabs in each channel that allow you to introduce interactivity and meet Teams' maximum potential by adding Apps to the tabs.

This function allows the instructor to integrate resources into your Team or Channel. This is a really cool innovation, and it will bring more productivity and creativity to the student's experience.

CHAPTER 3

USES AND IMPORTANCE OF MICROSOFT TEAM FOR EDUCATION AND BUSINESS

Connect Solutions survey showed 77% of remote workers report higher productivity when they work outside the organization. This is one of the benefits of the internet; we don't have to work on-site. Now emails, apps, records, etc. are available anywhere.

Recent world events such as COVID-19 have made it important that staff and their colleagues have access to their equipment, without being able to reach the workplace. Large businesses requested their staff to remain at home to reduce the virus' spread and risks.

This has contributed to a new challenge for companies: how to work efficiently. While Skype for Business has many features, including live conferences, it cannot fit all your team's needs. Let's assume that you would contact a certain community on a regular basis about a certain project; maybe you need to refer to emails to keep track of all that has been exchanged in that specific project.

Some apps, such as Slack, attempt to fill the gap and succeed. But irrespective of all Slack's fascinating activities, one thing remains, and that is protection. This is where teams from Microsoft come in.

Things You Should Know About Microsoft Teams

1) A Platform for Today's Teams

Microsoft Teams was created for today's diverse workforces. Over the years, corporate teams have undergone tremendous changes in the way they work and interact, conventional hierarchies giving way to flatter organizational structures, thus increasing the rapid dissemination of data and communication. Teams provide you with an open digital environment that allows you to work in-house, efficiently. Everything around you is still known with teams.

The three famous G's are at the heart of this and all other services offered by Office 365:

Governance – In order to protect applications and to fulfill different compliance criteria, features such as e-discovery are introduced.

Graphs – Everything you do inside the Office 365 Suite is recorded as a signal for the exploration of content in the applications.

Groups – Groups that are comprised of internal or external users may be set up in Office 365 Package, then they can work together with the same community to access items.

Teams are already part of the Microsoft Community so that all data and communications are accessible through the unified management and management console of Microsoft Graph and Office 365. Teams make it easier for you to integrate solutions – it is part of a robust platform.

A flexible conversation experience is provided by Microsoft Teams. You may enjoy continuous conversations via thread. Looking at this from a wider perspective, each interaction within Teams becomes information assets and is saved automatically. These assets can be searched via Microsoft Graph. These talks become available to every one of your team, but you can also open up private chats.

In addition, deep integration with Skype enables you to maximize your team members' interaction with video and speech, alongside a wide range of digital visual communications resources.

2) Improved Meeting Experience with Scheduling Capabilities

The ability to digitally reach businesses today is critical. Teams provides you with an outline of your planned meetings, the location, the subject, and a list of other participants.

3) Gallery of Bots

There are 24 bots available for improved efficiency with a number of functions. The T-Bot is the most basic and frequently asked team questions, Polly Bot for polling staff, Statsbot for scheduled reporting from sources like Salesforce and Google Analytics, and Growbot that allow you to share links with your employees.

4) The Ideal Teamwork Hub

You can experience the entire scope and width of Office 365, with software, including PowerPoint, Excel, Word, Calendar, OneNote, SharePoint, Delve, and Power BI, when you become an integral part of an Office 365 Community. Since teams were built to maximize Microsoft Graph's potential by using these products, the workgroups and teams will now share insights.

5) Calling for mobile audio and video

Teams are available on Android and iOS as well (audio only) and offer a simple, easy-to-use app that allows you to talk through text, speak or video call with your team.

6) Very customizable

Customization is an essential function of any application in this era. All organizations are unique. If you look for a way to improve your organization's commitment, the solution is Microsoft Teams. This latest method can be customized to fulfill both the organization's special business and cultural needs. Teams provide you with a forum with extensibility options and open widely accessible APIs. Teams will give you updates and alerts from third parties' services such as GitHub and Twitter using Microsoft Exchange's Connector model. With Microsoft's additional support, your company will build and configure applications and other resources to connect with the Microsoft Teams.

7) Improved protection

Protection is another environment where Microsoft teams stand apart and protect your safety. When you use one of the cloud features of Office 365, you will have state-of-the-art safety and enforcement capabilities. During transit and rest, your data is encrypted. Office 365 teams and all other service providers follow ISO 27001, HIPPA compliance requirements. The EU Model Clauses for SOC 2 teams are also part of Microsoft's global data center network and are said to be operational in a transparent manner. Office 365 offers the Staff account and handles it via the admin console.

Microsoft Teams will soon become a leading force in business relations and partnership. Don't miss the chance to join the campaign and increase the overall productivity. You can customize teams, groups, SharePoint, or any other Office 365 service to your needs once you understand the business problem you are trying to solve.

Why Educational Institutions NEED to Use Microsoft Teams

Since 2017, the availability of Microsoft Teams has increased for education institutions.

The training set for Microsoft teams varies slightly from the one for enterprises, as it provides even educational features, such as class-based notebooks, staff notebooks, and other educational apps or organizations. Office 365 is now free and harnesses the strength of its current investment by Microsoft teams.

So, is Microsoft teams really the perfect solution? For these main factors, many say it is:

1. Teamwork Service Core

Where Microsoft uses this language in the marketing campaign, Microsoft's teams are often viewed as being early in their own Office 365 journeys in higher education institutions. Microsoft Teams provide "unification of competitiveness," as they put it.

In some universities, professors and students can already use Office 365 core features for mail boxing and storing / sharing of information. Their use of Office 365 cannot, however, be more efficient than Microsoft Teams which allow users to leapfrog through those apps easily.

Instead, Microsoft teams can be opened easily by users of Office 365 for entry.

2. Today's Digital Natives are students and educators

When I began university in the mid-1990s, the school usually did not provide students with an email address. The dominant free email provider's email address is Hotmail at the moment. Before they go through the gates, the students already use new technology for their schooling and social life. As a consequence, they know and expect similar new technology to be used in their higher education life.

Students do not want conventional portals and emails that are based on the intranet. Chat services that connect them seamlessly with their teachers and peers but also integrate with other systems and apps can be extremely useful in schooling.

Microsoft Teams offers a single multipurpose platform to both students and teachers, which takes queues from traditional social elements when incorporating them into other resources and applications.

3. Preparing Students for the Real World

Although there are several leading strategies for handling education and creating open spaces, such as Moodle and Blackboard, institutions are mindful that the use of this technology ceases when students leave.

If students join the workforce, a summary of a job requirement would not include "familiarity with Microsoft Office." Rather, graduates could benefit from being equipped with collaboration tools from key players in the technology sector.

Most of this is Office 365, and it is critical that students already know the wider range of software and Microsoft teams.

Online learning can't replace classrooms. Microsoft Teams wants to change that

Online learning in most school districts is a breeze with the right technologies to support it. In the meantime, millions of students at home had to work through remote learning's numerous challenges.

Through its staff, Microsoft has seen tremendous success, albeit mostly in the corporate sector. Today, Microsoft announced a range of new features, especially in the field of student engagement, linked to remote learning.

New features support the digital transformation

Let's take a look at the recent changes in the last few months. Jarod Spataro, Microsoft 365 company vice president, shared a very shocking statistics in an online press briefing.

He said that Microsoft claims it has experienced nearly two years of digital transformation in two months of transitions to online learning and work. He noted that 70% of Microsoft Team meetings now are held for educational purposes.

Spataro said Microsoft wants to help users, researchers, and third-party experts to listen to, learn, and get insights.

Microsoft has created a new range of teams that will help students and employees communicate more easily by reducing the fatigue of remote education and meetings. This includes "Together Mode," an experience of team meetings created and published due to the pandemic's emergency.

I had to do it in a 14-person conference room. With one click, my meeting room's square video tiles changed to a feed where all participants were put in a virtual auditorium. I could see and check the other people on the call immediately. The chairs in an auditorium were overlaid as if we were seated in the same room.

Microsoft claims that this is ideal for brainstorming, seminars, and teaching because people will look to each other as they talk. I could note the tiny elements of the body language of others in the call, including smiles.

I felt like I was with them in the same room, and I could even pick up five people if I wanted. Microsoft says Together mode is less straining than standard video calls, and they're right. I was reassured by the encounter, which contrasts directly with the anxiety I get during video-conferencing.

Together Mode is one of many features that can create what Microsoft calls "blended learning," a combination of online community cooperation, recording lectures, and live lectures. It also helps to differentiate teams from Google Classroom, Zoom, and other programs.

Other features include "Dynamic View." The design of team screens shows what is more relevant in a more responsive and versatile way. Chat bubbles appear over video streams to make communication simpler and live reactions normal when chatting into a conference.

The challenges and science of online-learning

In Together Mode, Microsoft spilled a great deal of science analysis. To get to the bottom of it, I spoke to Microsoft's researcher Jaron Lanier.

Lanier said that you don't know where other people are on the screen while you are videoconferencing in grid mode. Together Mode solves that by establishing a collective space.

"The brain is capable of perceiving people naturally in a particular position," explained Lanier. "If someone is normally on the monitor, they seem to be rotated to their looks on the screen. This is attributable to an unacceptable look."

How did users respond to this? Lainer notes that his analysis indicates that the preliminary findings were extremely optimistic.

"I haven't yet met [any] who choose not to use [it]," Lanier said. "No professor who wanted to use it has stopped so far."

All this sounds good, as long as Microsoft is able to persuade schools to enroll. Education teams are also in operation in many school systems, including Florida's Duval County Public Schools. This includes free subscriptions from Microsoft 365, which are already charged by certain colleges.

Teams are getting features that go beyond education

Education teams have more than Together Mode. Microsoft also helps to streamline the teamwork, to improve the integration of meetings, and more.

This includes video filters for presentations, similar to those used in Snapchat and social media applications, a message extension for supervisors to track the well-being of workers, and a speech assignment for live subtitles and transcripts. Microsoft has also confirmed that team meetings would benefit up to 1,000 people.

Like Windows 10, Microsoft, Teams are an ever-changing commodity, and Microsoft always listens to feedback.

CHAPTER 4
CREATIVE WAYS OF USING MICROSOFT TEAMS

Microsoft Teams can be a crucial tool for home jobs. How well it performs for you depends, however, on how many of the main features you know and use and how many tricks you know.

Learning how to use the main features of the app, like joining a channel and posting a comment, is simple, particularly because the first time you use a team you get short tutorials.

Let's look instead at what's less clear. What follows is a series of 10 easy and effective tips that enable you to stay organized and to turn off some alerts to eliminate distractions. Read how Slack works and some alternatives to these two common Chat Apps to know more about Microsoft Teams.

1. Customize Notifications at the App Level

Team chat alerts help you keep up with relevant discussions, but those that are unimportant can be terrible distractions. Therefore, the customization of notifications is significant.

At the app-level, alerts can be configured for mentions, messages, and other account updates, for example, when someone enters or leaves. The only one you cannot totally disable is direct mentions of your username by others in chats.

To get there, in the upper right corner, press your profile button, select Settings, and select Alerts.

2. Customize Notifications at the Channel Level

Any channels you entered for fun and socialization or all channels you watch or listen to passively can be deactivated. Even when you turn off channel alerts, when there is a new activity, the channel's name always turns bold, letting you know you can fall in and catch up.

To get there, go over the name of the channel until there are three lines. Select Channel Notifications by clicking on the points.

3. Customize Notifications at the Conversation Level

You can switch off alerts entirely at the conversation stage (also known as a thread), which is helpful if a thread is going off the rails.

To hit the top right corner of the original post, hover over the reach string and three points. To toggle off alerts, click on the three lines. You can always get a warning if anyone mentions you even though updates are disabled.

4. Send a Private Chat Without Leaving a Channel

Microsoft teams keeps different channels and conversations. This is not helpful if you have to immediately send a message to someone privately during a channel conversation. However, there is a way.

Click the message profile of the user. A message field will pop up, which is simply a fast way to send a conversation.

5. Turn a conversation into a call to audio or video

The audio and video calling system is implemented in Microsoft teams. This allows the speaker's any interaction with a fellow Member to translate into a telephone call or video call. There is a range of ways to call your colleagues, including clicking the profile image and picking the calling icon. Another way is for a private conversation to turn into one call. This choice is convenient if text messaging is not as efficient as you want.

Click on the icon of the camera or on the phone in the top-right corner from your conversation. The app automatically dials the individual in the conversation.

6. Share your picture

It is easy to ask a colleague to look over your shoulder on your computer if you physically share office space with others. In a remote work environment, it is just as convenient to share your screen with your colleagues. You can start a call with somebody with Microsoft teams and then allow screen sharing.

Click on the sharing option in the lower part of the window once you start the call. Please be informed that a screen sharing administrator must allow it to run.

7. Add a virtual history to video calls

Perhaps you've seen all the fun background photos to Zoom virtual meetings that people have added. You can do this with Microsoft Teams as well, but you may think it does not offer you a convenient way to create your own image. However, that isn't true, and Lance Whitney explains in his tutorial how you can do it.

The short version of his guidance is to drop the image you want to use in a folder for the background picture choices of Microsoft teams.

8. Tidy Up Your Channel Bar

To begin with, pin the channels to the top of this region. Flip through the name of the channel until you see three lines. Choose Lock, press the lines.

Second, if appropriate, you can extend teams. The more teams that break down, the more the channel bar is structured.

Third, by dragging and lowering the teams, you can reposition them and increase the number of important teams.

9. Try / Orders

As a place to type commands, you double the search bar at the top of your Microsoft team browser. Commands help you to access the app more easily and efficiently. If you are not technically competent, commands can sound overwhelming, but they actually aren't.

Try to code the search bar with an advanced slash (/). There is a list of potential commands that you do not memorize. The software also allows you to complete the order. For example, the app automatically lets you type /chat to type the name of the person you want to send a message to.

Microsoft Teams Leader Attribution

Teams also provide students with live subtitles and transcripts of all skills, and we now add speaker attributions that will add speakers' names to the subtitles. When a lecture is finished, a complete transcript can be downloaded and stored, with a simple reference as to who has said what. And the overall number of participants in the class has been raised to accommodate classes that occupy the biggest lecture halls on the campus. Teams can allow 1,000 participants to connect with audio, video, and talk in a single meeting.

CHAPTER 5

BEST APPS AND STRATEGIES

Apps

- Flipgrid

- Wakelet

- Nearpod

- Pear deck

- Planner

Strategies

- Give Titles to Chat Exchanges.

- Use SharePoint to Share and Store Files.

- Forward Emails into Channels.

- Stick with Just a Few Groups at a Time.

- Test Your Communications Strategies

Flipgrid

As we all know, the video-sharing app Flipgrid is popular in schools — so popular in so many countries that "Flipgrid Fever" can be attributed to its rapid growth. This app has been free to use by educators since it was purchased by Microsoft for over a year now.

The simple use of Flipgrid is one of the key advantages. Teachers create an account and set up networks in which students operate as groups. The instructor generates inspiring threads in each grid, and the students post videos on the directions and answers to each other. Most of the videos are very brief, just a minute or two long, and the tool is very easy for children to use.

Flipgrid's new features

1. Sharing book reviews: The latest Augmented Reality function of Flipgrid lets students exchange book reviews with the classrooms, and classroom libraries use the video QR app. Once a student has recorded their analysis, the professor can print QR codes and tape them on the book, and classmates can check the code using their computers to use the analysis as a way of helping people determine if they would like to read the book.

2. Practicing language skills: Flipgrid helps teachers to work together in multiple districts and countries. This provides opportunities for world language teachers to practice their speakers with a wider audience than their classrooms. Students can upload videos and use their vocabulary and can share their skills with other students worldwide who speak the same language or talk to native speakers of another language instead of being restricted to communicating with people in their physical classroom.

3. Functionality for all students is increasing: Flipgrid has extended several of its functionality to allow all students to take part. Closed captions may be used by students while watching videos, which often produce a complete transcript for each video. For both

closed captions and any text in style, Microsoft Immersive Reader can be used to read texts aloud and separate words in syllables to make them easier to decipher.

4. Inviting external speakers: Teachers are encouraged to engage in classroom conversations using guest mode. Student videos and their own videos are open to visitors. This enables experts in one area to share their expertise asynchronously with students who post videos of their questions to help the expert answer a video response conveniently. For instance, STEM teachers may invite engineers or scientists to speak and answer student's questions about their careers and study.

5. Building portfolios for students: a teacher can create a portfolio for students. The instructor creates a subject in this grid for each student, and students post videos describing their work, showcasing an ability that has just been studied or reflecting on classroom experience. The teacher should share with the student's parents and guardians his connection to the subject to allow them to see the work of their child all year round. Since the subjects can also be made accessible to each student, they can watch the work of their classmates.

6. Adding annotations: when students record a video, they can write on the video directly and add additional text to a sticky note. This feature is a great way to demonstrate your reasoning for math students who practice solving problems or chemistry students who can learn to solve chemical equations.

7. Build a mixtape: The mixtape is a way to curate videos on a single location from any subject or map. An instructor can choose any student video that is shared with the entire class by adding it to the mix. Gathering year-round memories is an excellent way of using this feature: as the year advances, teachers can save interesting videos or important moments from various subjects. The mixtape will help students understand what they learned at the end of the year.

8. Sharing and celebrating work: The time constraints often make it forgotten to celebrate assignments or finished jobs in school, but Flipgrid makes this simple and quick. Everyone in the class can view and respond to each other's videos using the student-to-student answering option. For example, students in a history class may share a long-term project they have accomplished through studying and developing. Class peers can write video comments, with constructive reviews on the completed work.

9. Students help the absent ones: Flipgrid can be a catch-up option for missing students. The teacher creates a subject for classwork, and, when a student is away during a certain period, one of her or his colleagues will post a short video about the tasks in the classroom in order to quickly allow the absent students to learn what they missed.

Wakelet

Wakelet is a way to bookmark, organize and curate content from across the web and use it to create beautiful, informative and engaging collections.

Submit a student information center

It is easier to divert your students from the internet if you need to write a job or plan for a class debate. By searching a collection of resources in Wakelet, you can make sure your students get info from a platform that contains quality information and not get distracted or confused with poorly searched articles and fake news.

Enable collaboration of students in group projects

Combining Wakelet and teams encourages students to work in collaboration with the rest of the class to create community projects that they can share. Create a community collection on Wakelet and invite students to use links across the site, PDFs, photos, and text to add their own content. You can then just select 'Share teams' or use the Wakelet app in teams to display it and add your own thoughts and suggestions from the rest of the class.

Share the team's strengths and ideas

Good ideas are worth sharing! Why not curate a list of wakelets full of helpful tools, regardless of whether you've found the idea of great course design, a creative way of approaching a certain subject, or an outline for a conference? In the departments, you may then easily apply this to your offices, the whole faculty, or your PLN. It is also a perfect way to ensure Participants who are missing events – seminars, webinars, lectures, and more – can catch up with those who have attended.

Simplify your six-month strategy

It's easy to end up swamped with infinite Tablers, Presents and instructions if your team or department prepares for the year or semester ahead. You can streamline the process and store it all in one location with Wakelet. You can upload documents as pdf-files, create a portfolio to share with your colleagues in teams, add Web-language links, photos, tweets, and more. From a set of SEL tools to the ideas for Minecraft lessons!

Nearpod

It is simply that the team or department gets prepared for the year or semester to come with endless tablers, presents, and instructions. With Nearpod, all of this can be simplified and saved in one place. Documents can be downloaded as pdf files, and a portfolio shared between teams, weblinks, photographs, tweets, and more.

How to shake Nearpod in that presentation

You will need to be sure that you log in and have already built an account on Nearpod for your Microsoft Teams account. Click the "+" sign at the top right of the tab bar from your favorite team's "General" window.

You will be told what kind of tab you want to add once you click on the "+" button. You can scan for it easily if Nearpod does not appear in the first few pages. Go on and click on the Nearpod screen until it shows up.

You will now be required to log into your account of nearby

educators. Sign in and enter your username, then press "Check-in" blue. Tip: It seems like you will have no choice for logging in at first glance.

The presentation will automatically integrate directly into your Teams channel once you've selected your preferred lesson form. The dialogue will also appear in the top tab row. You have incorporated your presentation in teams effectively!

How to interrupt The Microsoft live class session

Click on the "camera" icon at the bottom of your toolbar to start a live class meeting in Microsoft Teams. If you are uncertain about what icon you want to select, try floating over them before you find the one that says "meet now." You are LIVE now!

How to start your Nearpod presentation

You will have to wait until your students log on to the meeting now that you are Offline. Clicking on the "Participants" icon (which looks like two people), you can verify the attendance of the meeting. Upon one's arrival, tell your students that you will be working together on a Nearpod demonstration. Display that you'll have to press the Back button in your meet team window. Explain that you can use either the post in the chat or the tab atop to access the Nearpod presentation. You will be asked to log in using your name once you pick Nearpod. You can start your live lesson once all of you have logged in!

Pear Deck

Pear Deck is an amazing tool that enables teachers or students to create interactive activities. It can be used with Google and Microsoft, and we will examine how it can be used by PowerPoint and Microsoft Teams below.

Students quickly answer questions by joinpd.com and enter a join code. You can do it from any computer quickly.

Classroom suggestions for the use of pear decks

Pear Deck is a compliment to something you know and love already, PowerPoint or Google Slides. This means there's no need for a new platform to learn, and you don't have to build another platform. Pear Deck allows for formative evaluation, learning, and relevant knowledge on student education and development to be quickly gathered!

We must all get material out to children, but what matters is how we do it. Students have to take part in the process because the student who works is the one who learns.

To that end, it is time to learn to update and interactively use Pear Deck so students are dedicated, and the instructor can also review their perspectives and content simultaneously!

Have a platform for students and let them explore

- Send: allow students to share ideas with others in long or short replies — and then display the reactions on the computer, if possible, to help students learn from each other's ideas.

- Drag feature: students should pull a dot or a pin to illustrate their meaning.

- Have student solve mathematics problems or demonstrate blood flow in the heart. You give them the start-their imagination and learning will follow.

- Multiple choice-search quickly with reply options.

- The best thing is that students can describe their thoughts and discuss their ideas through Pear Deck.

Planner

You will want to consider how emerging innovations might aid your department in preparing your marketing campaign this year. A simple, easy to use project management tool that can be integrated with Microsoft Teams and MS Office 365 can be used by Microsoft Team Manager. The Microsoft team planner can be used to include some of the functions that your company is looking for in order to find a better way of organizing and managing its marketing policies.

In addition to the advantages of integration into the Microsoft Office 365 platform, these are some of the advantages of the Microsoft team manager.

What is Microsoft Planner?

Microsoft Planner is a tool for task and project management that can be incorporated directly with Microsoft Teams and other MS

Office products. In an all-in-one dashboard that can then be shared between team members, Microsoft Planner provides an easy-to-use summary of tasks to complete. The planner's purpose as an organizational tool is to help workers work together, organize all their information, and keep it clear and transparent. The team members can discuss tasks, communicate, and chat about projects and tasks through the Microsoft Team Planner. The planner can be accessed from anywhere as a cross-platform app and is accessible on desktops, cell phones, and other devices. Email alerts and the flexibility of Microsoft Teams ensure that team members do not miss crucial tasks and that all of them are still on the same page.

The Microsoft team manager makes coordination and collaboration simpler for marketing strategists with various marketing teams and departments. Team members in the planner will track multiple marketing campaigns, divide into easy steps per project, and ensure all team members are aware of the objectives and tasking for which they are responsible.

Why join teams and managers in Microsoft?

Although Microsoft Planner can be used as an individual product, planners can be integrated into the Microsoft Team Platform with many benefits. The Microsoft Teams network offers chat channels and chat rooms one by one to connect with members of MS teams inside Office 365.

See clearly what other members of the team do. Marketing teams need to work successfully together. Through the convergence of the two systems, team members can quickly see the tasks and projects assigned to each other.

Attribute team roles. Marketing teams also work concurrently on many tactics and campaigns. Microsoft teams allow fast implementation and tracking of Microsoft Planner projects and activities, with each team member aware of its projects.

Act on projects more effectively. Marketing departments have to study and consult on various materials and media regularly. Microsoft's combination of the Microsoft Planner and Microsoft Teams makes it simple, through attachments, notes, and integrated files, to discuss, exchange, and change these documents in real-time.

The Microsoft team planner connections to Microsoft teams are similar to connecting the Microsoft calendar to Microsoft teams: they allow team planning from within the Microsoft team platform to be managed, controlled and maintained.

Integrating Microsoft Planner with Teams

By adding a planner tab to the Microsoft team interface, you can easily incorporate Microsoft Planner into Microsoft teams. Select "Add Tab" on the Microsoft Teams page. "Planner" can be seen to be selected on the "Add Tab" panel.

If the Microsoft Planner is chosen, a new Microsoft Team tab will be added. This tab can be accessed by team members and can be updated directly inside the Dashboard of Microsoft Teams.

Add "work." Each work is covered by a bucket, and each bucket is to be split into small, convenient measures.

Tasks can then be delegated to team members directly once they have been established. Team members will be informed of the assignment of a task. In the meantime, you will modify the role with:

Set status and date for the task

Prioritizing the task, including the degree of design priority

To better define the task, you need to add checklists, explanations, and attachments

Every role can be addressed with team members on the Microsoft Teams dashboard, and these discussions are saved from being easily checked. This makes working together simpler and for large teams in the whole Microsoft, Teams ecosystem to work together and interact effectively.

The planner is a valuable complement to every marketing campaign, combined with Microsoft teams. Now is the time to turn to Microsoft teams if you want to develop your marketing technologies.

CHAPTER 6
PROS AND CONS

S ince its launch in 2017, Microsoft Teams has come a long way. The modern age has further stressed Microsoft's name for online collaboration. Many organizations still use teams as an official tool for teamwork in their organization, and others have recently turned to teams to support their remote workers.

But for those of you who have not made a final decision about teams, we listed some advantages and disadvantages. If you want to know how teams compare similar goods, this is our recent comparison between Microsoft Teams versus Slack versus Zoom.

Key Elements

You first have to consider their key components to consider the benefits and drawbacks of teams.

Equipment

All begins with a team. Create a team from scratch or use your new team from an existing Microsoft 365 community. Then, invite people you want to work with.

Networks

In general, networks are communications between you and other team members. Like Slack, a team, project, or subject can be created on channels. They are a place for chatting, holding meetings, adding files, and working with people.

Windows Tabs

Tabs help you browse the content of your site. You've got three tabs by default: blogs, folders, and wikis. Their names are simple — Each chat you have is stored in the Posts tab, while the Files tab stores all the documents you share with people in the forum. The Wiki tab is an insightful text editor for publishing, posting, and chatting. If you like, you can add more personalized or streamlined tabs.

Pros

Microsoft Teams has the advantage of integrating all other cooperation software and instruments from Microsoft 365. Teams can be used as a central hub using the functionality of many applications, including Planner, Outlook, and SharePoint, without having to exit the system interface. Here's more details on the benefits of Microsoft Teams:

1. No additional cost for Microsoft 365 users

Some businesses can find increased costs a deal-breaker. And remember, teams' feature won't cost you a single dime if your business already has a Microsoft 365 license. On the other hand, standalone chat tools such as Slack or Google Hangouts may mean an extra cost to your business. Also, you can always use a free version of teams if you do not need premium features.

2. A useful addition to chat

In your platforms, you can install third-party software. Using Teams doesn't mean that you have to abandon other instruments that you usually use. You may also incorporate storage services such as Google Drive or Dropbox, for example.

Many fun options, including emoticons, gifs, and sticks, are also offered. It might not sound like a lot, but emoticons can really make your workday easier.

3. Finding, backup, and cooperation seamless data

There is separate file storage for each track. If you have to scroll to find a particular file, the file tabs are helpful — you don't have to click through all the channels.

You have a fair chance of finding some old documents that you shared with a team months ago given you did some backups. Also, you won't lose the files even if you delete a channel on a SharePoint website.

You should move this document to a different tab if you are actually working on a significant document to differentiate it from other documents. As we mentioned above, you can work on a file in real-time, without leaving the chat.

4. Nice bots

Bots will help and save you some time on your dull daily tasks. You can build them for yourself or use them as they are.

A bot behaves like every other team member you communicate

with except that it is always online with a hexagonal avatar icon.

Cons

Even if teams are a great tool for Microsoft, users will still fight with the lack of some features. Some of the drawbacks for Microsoft teams that we faced during its use are described below.

1. There are so many common tools

Ironically, some Microsoft tools represent the main stumbling block for teams. With a multitude of choices, people are quite bewildered as to what method to use. It is Microsoft's duty to educate its users on their software.

2. No single product quest

Although Microsoft suggests that teams should be used to perform special team talks and Yammer to report on general business, both platforms are still used interchangeably.

3. Required storage consumption

Everyone in the community will build a team by default. This can contribute to needless team building and storage space. The good news is that a number of users will limit their permission to build a team. First, you must create a distinct security community for the people you want to construct teams and then run a few PowerShell commands.

4. Notices were incomplete

If you want to create a new team with the same name, you will not get a notification, so that you may get confused with other existing teams.

This problem has a solution though, before you start a new team, you can see if the team name is already taken in the search bar by entering the name. A list of all the current teams will be given, and the name will not be duplicated.

5. There are a few channels

There are 200 public and 30 private channels per team. The number is limited to 30. While for smaller organizations, it might not be a concern; others may be need more. You will have to delete some channels if you reach this limit. Please note that common files remain as backup storage in the SharePoint database.

In the 1990s, and since then, the idea of instant messaging has revolutionized our way of communicating. More than 3 billion people are now projected to use one message application daily on leasing.

Microsoft Teams has revolutionized not only the way we deliver the message, but also reached new heights of collaboration with features like the threaded conversations, video, and voice conferencing, and the exchange of files and documents. This week alone, Microsoft has released a preview of Microsoft's Linux teams, which is noteworthy because it's the first open-source Operating system.

The benefits of Microsoft Teams

Contact streamlined

Teams allow users to improve efficiency by making all their communication accessible in a single app or GUI – messages, calls, online meetings, shared files, projects, and so forth. The Microsoft teams chat feature enables users to conduct discussions in a single, easily findable location, enabling users to store brainstorming sessions, conferences, and other meetings.

Microsoft Teams Continues To Roll Out New Features

As we discussed in the Inspire 2020 study, after the COVID-19 pandemic started and forced several workers to operate on a monthly basis, Microsoft has continued to introduce new features. With the SPOTOL choice, organizers of meetings and presenters can lock their video to help the presenter track the main video feed that is used during a meeting. Call Merge allows users to combine a variety of calls into one 1-1 or a separate community call.

Increased Productivity

We are tired of hearing how any new app on the market "builds efficiency," but what does this mean? When you're talking using Microsoft teams, you're making sure no team member loses a major conversation or modified document when anyone forgets to press "Reply to all." In teams, everyone gets the same message exactly at the same time, so everyone can communicate and keep discussions.

If you plan to appoint a new team member to a project, the new member will have access to all the previous discussions and shared information.

Integrate All Office 365 Applications

Teams should not only restrict users to the features of chat/contact. It enables users to fold any Office 365 applications. This ensures that teams can display and edit the same presentation in real-time for Text, Excel, or PowerPoint.

Advantages

1: Clearer focus on the project

Microsoft teams can work quickly on particular assignments and help you manage your time more efficiently and give priority to tasks.

In order to make it like you can only see messages, papers, and requests for meeting on a specific platform, Microsoft Teams break information into selected channels. You have less risk of being disturbed via meaningless conversations or by cleaning a messy inbox.

Rather, Microsoft teams will quickly focus on the job at hand, showing only basic tools relevant to the work that you do.

2: Improved efficiency contact

The wide variety of collaboration tools available on the system will make navigation challenging, as reported by Office 365 users.

Through incorporating all projects in a single system and app, Microsoft teams improving employee efficiency – including assignments, shared data, meetings, conversations, and more. Many 'outside' applications are also compatible with teams, so users don't have to leave the team app to do their job.

3: Closer Interactions

Several organizations find it difficult to keep employees up to date with the latest changes in the company and to ensure that the situation is transparent to all relevant workers.

Microsoft teams simplify life greatly, eliminating the difficulty of adding a cc to an email or an invitation to a meeting. Teams is very good at simply posting the message on the correct platform, by indicating whoever is essential for discussion or meeting, whereas other appropriate staff can see and decide, if necessary, to respond to the message. As a consequence, contact is much more straightforward.

4: New workers fast integration

With the versatility of today's workplace and the ever-growing opportunity to work remotely for workers, applicants can be found all over the world.

If you choose the right person for the job, Microsoft Teams will eliminate all the stress from the starting process. If the organization is based in the nation, the platform ensures easy and smooth incorporation into the teamwork framework.

5: Smooth transition to the digital workspace

The transition to a digital workspace in the cloud offers a range of advantages. The switch to that sort of platform may not be any simpler than with Microsoft Teams, which itself is a totally cloud-based collaboration solution.

The ability to access all relevant information on any type of computer anywhere in the world is one of the main business advantages of switching to a digital workspace. In addition, massive data processing and artificial intelligence tasks can be carried out easily, allowing the entire workforce to work smarter and to increase efficiency in the organization.

Disadvantages

1: Uncertain structure

Most of us nowadays just look for a title and deliver what we need; we just couldn't care less about "where" files are stored physically on our systems.

But Microsoft teams are maybe less than optimal for those who still place priority over file placement. The file structure may be considered confusing as all chat uploads transfer to the root folder of the site. In an effort, the file links inside the conversations breaking down by moving them into properly named files.

2: Change from Complicated Outlook

It is best for all team members to fully commit to the platform and abandon the use of Outlook, even in the case of external correspondence, to ensure a smoothest possible transition to Microsoft teams.

Since Office 365 still has many other features depending on Outlook, it can be hard to avoid using the tool.

For example, at the time of writing, Teams do not support Group calendars, and Word document links cannot be sent via a Team chat.

3: Permission difficulties

One of Microsoft's main benefits is the simplicity of the process in which files and documents are exchanged.

Automatic access to any required file, channel, and OneNote notebook should be accessible for all team members.

This is ideal in principle, but it's not as straightforward to function together effectively and conveniently. In an ideal situation, you want to add permission settings to certain files that are not possible with Microsoft teams at the time of writing.

4: Engaged experience in the online meeting

The initiative by Microsoft to incorporate Skype for Business' smooth meeting features into its Microsoft team platform is unquestionable.

Overall, they have performed very well and have incorporated quite some additional features.

This said, however, the online meeting experience still leaves much to be desired – there is no insight, and some of the best-selling points in the entire team meeting center, including OneNote's billing functionality, are not promoted.

5: Restricted versatility potential manual duplications

You will not have the framework planned from the beginning by using Microsoft Teams. You won't know the networks are needed and what teams are needed for development.

Over time, you can become more conscious by using the app more often and by becoming more conscious of what tasks it helps you with most.

In their current incarnation, Microsoft teams' building blocks lack versatility in some way – they cannot replicate networks or teams. Therefore, manual repetition can be a necessary yet time-consuming activity.

6: Some users can find the file structure confusing

You can find teams a bit confusing if you are one of those users who always want to know where a file is located in a folder structure (including looking for everything you need). Everything in the teams that is uploaded to conversations is dumped in the root folder of the site, so if you try to organize the files into properly named directories, the conversation links are broken.

7: Adding members

In comparison to Slack, where you can invite a user without having to worry, this move is not made simple by teams. Essentially there are two methods: native or guest access, and you must take a number of steps to ensure that you give external users the right permissions during the installation.

The Pros and Cons of Microsoft Teams vs. Zoom

There are a few different things you must consider when discussing the topic of Microsoft Teams vs. Zoom. Many of these have to do with a single organizational profile and what they expect from every platform.

Conferences

If your main objective is to use conference apps, then there are strong conference features on both platforms. Microsoft teams doesn't use an IT-professional and need an additional license to use the dial-in number from the box.

It does not also carry out major "live" webinars and requires a further license and configuration. Zoom conducts both wide conferences, and it has dial-in capabilities. It is a simple license upgrade that does not require an IT professional if you need to expand your max webinar limit.

Working together

Microsoft teams have advanced tools to support this process if you collaborate primarily with the software. Zoom does not really include such advanced collaboration features and cannot, therefore, be recommended as appropriate software. In addition to direct messaging and collaborative contact, Microsoft Teams has devoted spaces to interactions and cooperation with external networks.

Microsoft's Cloud Management Platform also includes Microsoft 365 teams who take full advantage of the online Word, Excel, and PowerPoint. With OneDrive and SharePoint, it can also be incorporated directly online. There's no end to the integrations! Microsoft teams may be combined to provide end-users with a wide variety of different applications. Imagine your whole job in a single application!

Security

Let's discuss the security of the two sites since this subject has been covered in a lot of news, namely Zoom. Whilst Zoom protection concerns were raised, many of these were reported as COVID-19 countries shut down in March 2020. Zoom worked rapidly to improve its protection features and made its efforts clear. Zoom had no major security problems at any time, and much of that was wasted as sensationalism.

There are securities holes in every application, whether they have been found or not. It is important to realize that both products are mature business applications with plenty of safety resources. A team of more than 3500, alongside advanced AI Systems, employs Microsoft alone to monitor and maintain product integrity.

CONCLUSION

In summary, Microsoft Teams' main disadvantages are major problems identified by the technological giant that is still being developed. Fortunately, they will not prove to be too much a problem in the future.

Particularly in the early stages after a switch, users may have several problems adapting to Microsoft Teams.

But the reward will be obvious if you make the necessary attempt to change your way of working with the new communication technology.

If a simple web conference tool is what your business need, it's not on Office 365, or if you want to avoid additional cost and complexity, Zoom is the right option for you. With Office 365 in your organization to enhance communication, partnership, and efficiency, Microsoft Teams is the best choice. Some companies will opt for both platforms due to the additional costs and complexity of establishing all additional conference functions for teams.

Printed in Great Britain
by Amazon

55357670R00047